T0083140

Zanaida Stewart Robles

MAGNIFICAT AND NUNC DIMITTIS

SATB | PIANO AND ORGAN

VOCAL SCORE

OXFORD
UNIVERSITY PRESS

OXFORD
UNIVERSITY PRESS

Great Clarendon Street, Oxford OX2 6DP,
United Kingdom

Oxford University Press is a department of the University of Oxford.
It furthers the University's objective of excellence in research, scholarship,
and education by publishing worldwide. Oxford is a registered trade mark of
Oxford University Press in the UK and in certain other countries

© Oxford University Press 2023

Zanaida Stewart Robles has asserted her right under the Copyright, Designs
and Patents Act, 1988, to be identified as the Composer of this Work

First published 2023

Impression: 1

All rights reserved. No part of this publication may be reproduced,
stored in a retrieval system, or transmitted, in any form or by any means,
without the prior permission in writing of Oxford University Press

Permission to perform this work in public (except in the course of divine worship)
should normally be obtained from a local performing right licensing organization,
unless the owner or the occupier of the premises being used already holds
a licence from such an organization. Likewise, permission to make and
exploit a recording of this work should be obtained from a
local mechanical copyright licensing organization

Enquiries concerning reproduction outside the scope of the above
should be directed to the Music Rights Department, Oxford University Press,
at music.permissions.uk@oup.com or at the address above

ISBN 978-0-19-356329-2

Music and text origination by Andrew Jones
Printed in Great Britain on acid-free paper by
Halstan & Co. Ltd, Amersham, Bucks.

Composer's note

My Magnificat and Nunc Dimittis were originally scored for SATB choir with both piano and organ accompaniment, as presented here. The piano and organ combination is a nod to the Black American church in which I grew up, where both instruments were used simultaneously for almost all music during church services (typically gospel music). All Saints Episcopal Church in Pasadena, California, for which my Magnificat and Nunc Dimittis were composed, also had a tradition of using both piano and organ with various styles for special occasions. Because of my study and work in the Episcopal church, my Magnificat and Nunc Dimittis are firmly rooted in the Western classical music tradition, heavily influenced by the works of Howells, Vaughan Williams, and Holst. The harmony, form, and melodic elements in both pieces employ heavy usage of the octatonic scale: an 8-note scale constructed by alternating semitones/half steps and tones/whole steps.

This note may be reproduced as required for programme notes.

Duration: Magnificat 5.5 minutes; Nunc Dimittis 6 minutes

This piece is also available in a version for SATB and organ only (ISBN 978–0–19–356507–4).

Magnificat

Luke 1: 46–55

ZANAIDA STEWART ROBLES

Duration: 5.5 mins

© Oxford University Press 2023. Photocopying this copyright material is ILLEGAL.

8
spi - rit hath re-joiced in God my Sa - viour. For he hath re-
11
-gard - ed the low - li-ness of his hand - maid.
Ped.
14
SOPRANOS & ALTOS unis.
mp
S./A.
For be-hold from hence - forth all ge-ne-ra - tions shall call me bless - ed,
p

18
S.
A.
for be - hold, from hence - forth all ge - ne - ra - tions
for be - hold, from hence - forth all ge - ne - ra - tions shall call me
For be - hold, from hence - forth all ge - ne - ra - tions
mp
T.
B.
mp
For be - hold, from hence - forth all ge - ne - ra - tions shall call me
legato
mp
shall call me bless - - - - ed.
f
21
bless - - - - - - ed.
shall call me bless - - - - ed.
f
bless - - - - - - ed.
f
p misterioso
f
p misterioso

25
mp
S.
For he that is might-y hath mag - - ni-fied
p
A.
Mag - - ni - fi - - cat a - -
p
T.
B.
Mag - - ni - fi - - cat a - -
29
me and ho - ly is his name.
- ni - ma me - - a,
- ni - ma me - - a,

33
(mp)
And his mer - cy is on them that fear
p
mag - - ni - fi - cat a -
p
mag - - ni - fi - cat a -
37
him through-out all ge - ne - ra - tions.
- ni - ma me - a.
- ni - ma me - a.
Man.

41
accel.
Allegro ♩ = 120
p
mf
mf
3
46
S.
A.
T.
B.
mp marcato
He hath shown strength
p marcato
He hath shown strength with his arm, he hath scat - tered the proud in the i -
p
3
mp
3
p
mp
Ped.

49
mf marcato
He hath shown strength with his arm, he hath
with his arm, he hath scat-tered the proud in the i - ma - gi - na - tion of their
mf
-ma - gi - na - tion of their hearts. Mag - ni - - fi - cat
mf
mf
52
scat-tered the proud in the i - ma - gi - na - tion of their hearts.
mf
hearts. Mag - ni - - fi - cat, he hath scat-tered the proud in the i -
mf marcato
He hath shown strength with his arm,
a - ni - - ma me - - a. He hath put down the might-

55
He hath put down the might-
-ma - gi - na - tion of their, He hath put down the might - y from their seat and
He hath put down the might - y from their seat and hath ex - alt - ed the
- y from their seat and hath ex - alt - ed the hum - - ble and
58
- y from their seat and hath ex - alt - ed the hum - - ble and
hath ex - alt - ed the hum - - ble and meek. Mag - ni -
hum - - ble and meek. Mag - ni - - fi - cat
meek. Mag - ni - - fi - cat a - ni - - ma

61
meek. Mag - ni - fi - cat. He hath fill - ed the hun - gry with
- fi - cat. He hath fill - ed the hun - gry with
a - ni - ma me - - a. He hath fill - ed the hun - gry with
me - a. He hath fill - ed the hun - gry with
65
S.
A.
good things and the rich he hath sent emp - ty a - way.
T.
B.

69
mf
He re - mem - ber-ing his mer - cy
mf
mer - - -
mf
mf
73
hath holp-en his ser - vant Is - ra - el as he pro - mised
-cy hath holp - en his ser - vant Is - ra - el as he

77
f
to our fore - fa - thers, A - bra - ham and his seed for
f
pro - mised to our fore - - fa - thers, A - bra - ham, for
f
f
80
ritard.
Majestically ♩ = 60
p
ev - - - er!
p
ev - - - er!
ritard.
Majestically ♩ = 60
8va
p
mp

84
mf
Glo - ry be to the Fa - ther, and to the Son, and to the Ho - ly Spi - rit;
mf
mf
mf

88
as it was in the be-gin - ning, is now and for ev-er shall be,
mp

92
mp
world with - out end, world with - out end, world with - out end,
mp
mp

96
world with - out end, world with - out end, world with - out end.
mp

rit.
100
A - (a) - - men, a - - - men, a -
p
A - men, a - men, a - - men,
p
A - (a) - men, a - - - men, a -
rit.
p
p
- - men,
a - - men, a - - - men.
a - - men,
- - men, a - men.
Tranquillo ♩ = 52
103
Tranquillo ♩ = 52
8va

Nunc Dimittis

Luke 2: 29–32

Duration: 6 mins

12
to thy word.
S.
A.
p
Ac - cord - ing to thy word.
T.
B.
p
16
unis.
p
S./A.
Lord, now let - - test thou thy
21
ser - vant de - part in peace, ac -

25
S.
A.
word.
- cord - ing to thy word, ac - cord - ing to thy
T.
B.
p
Ac - cord - ing to thy

29
word.
word.
ALTOS
p
For mine eyes have seen thy sal -

33
A.
-va - tion,
For mine eyes have seen thy sal -
mp
T.
B.
p
For mine eyes have seen thy sal - va - tion,
mp
mp

SOPRANOS
37
mp
S.
For mine eyes have seen thy sal - va - tion,
- va - tion,
mf
T.
B.
For mine eyes have seen thy sal -
mf
mf

41
mf
S.
A.
For mine eyes have seen
thy sal - va - tion be - fore the
T.
B.
- va - tion,
45
f
face of all peo - - ple.
f
f
f

49
To be a light to

53
light - en the Gen - tiles, And to be the
Ped.
Man.

57
mp
glo - ry, to be the glo - ry, the
mp
mp
Ped.
61
cresc.
glo - - ry of thy peo - - - - - ple
cresc.
mp cresc.

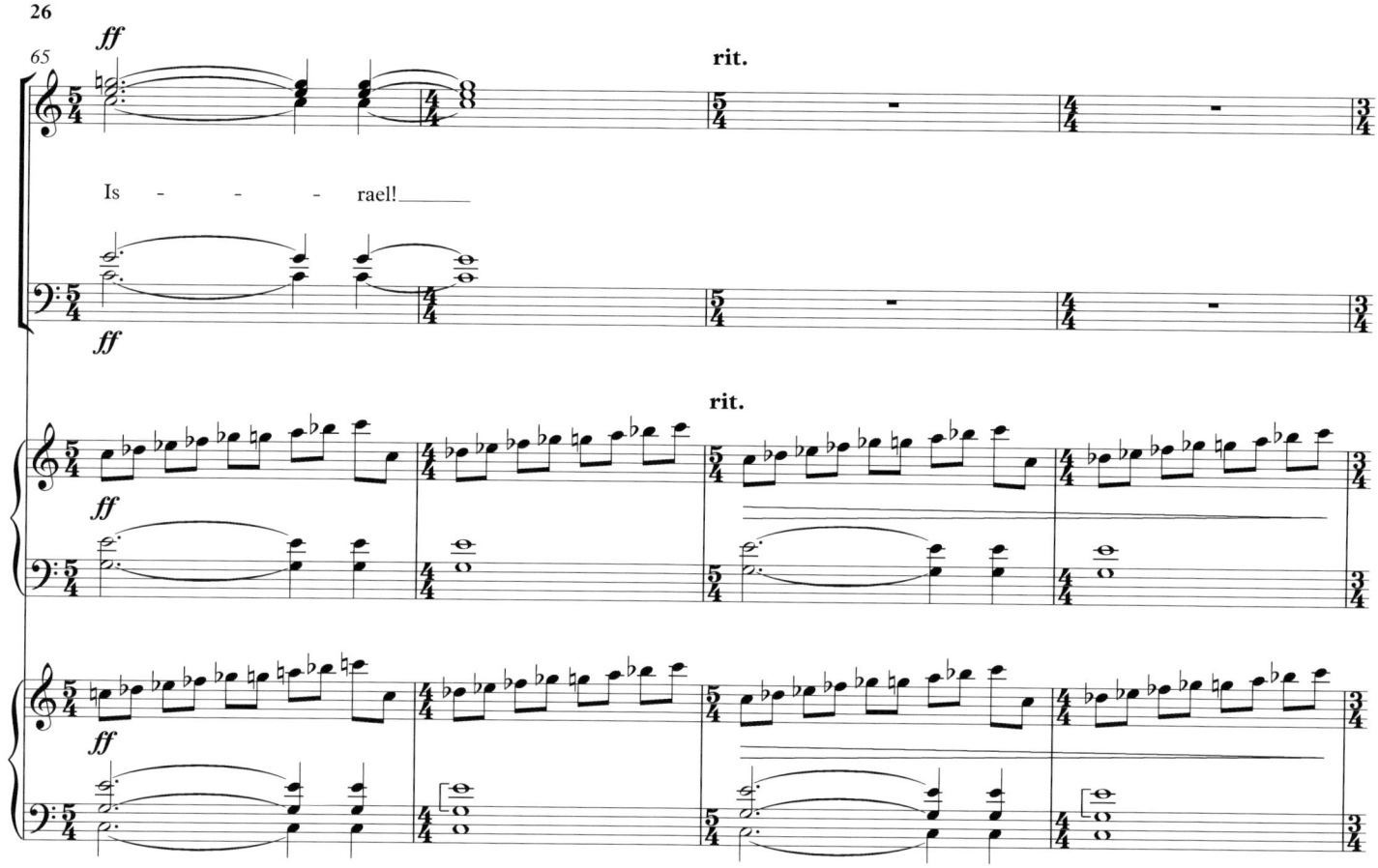
65
ff
rit.
Is - - - rael!
ff
rit.
ff
ff

69
Andante ♩ = 80
unis. mp
Glo - - ry be to the
unis.
mp
Andante ♩ = 80
p
p

73
Son, and
Fa - ther, and to the to the Ho - - ly
Son, and

77
As it
Spi - rit; was in the be -
As it

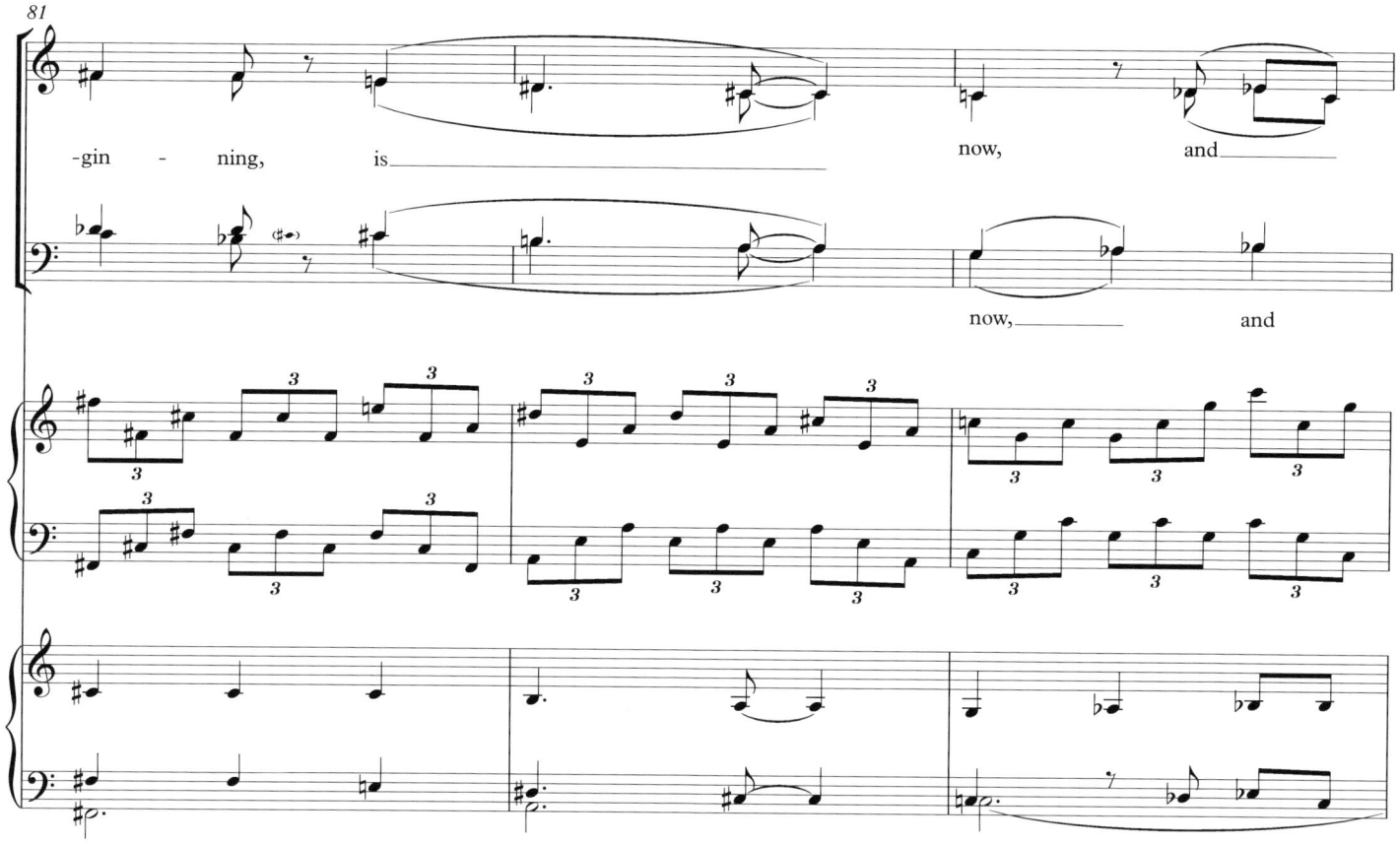
81
-gin - ning, is now, and
now, and

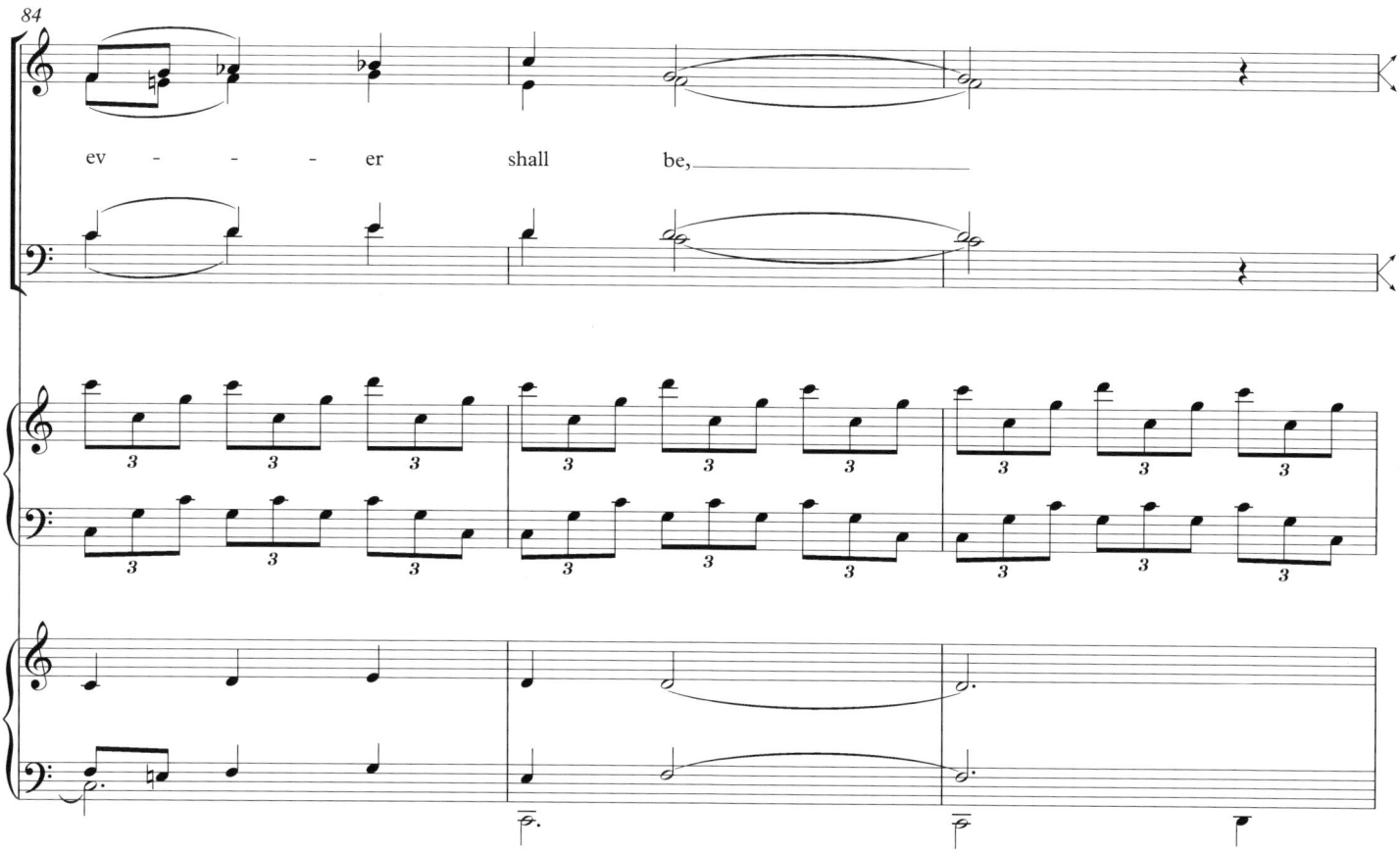
84
ev - - - er shall be,

87
S.
mf
world with - out
A.
mf
world with - out end, world with - out
T.
mf
world with - out
B.
mf
world with - out end, world with - out
mp
mp

91
end, world with - out
end, world with - out end,
end, world with - out
end, world with - out end,

95
f
end,
world with - out
f
world with - out
f
end,
world with - out
f
world with - out
mf
mf

99
end, world with - out end, world with - out
end, world with - out end, world with -
end, with - out end, world with - out
end, world with - out end, world with -

103
end.
A - - - - - - -
- out end.
A - - - men,
end.
A - - - - - - -
- out end.
A - - - - - - -
f
f

107
mf
men,
a
a
men,
men,
a
mf
men,
a
mf
mf

111
mp
men,
a
mf
a
men,
mf
men,
a
mp
men,
a
mp
mp

115
p
men,
a
mp
a
men,
mp
p
men,
a
p
men,
a
p
p

119
rit.
men,
a men,
men,
men,
rit.
Tranquillo ♩ = 70
p
123
S.
A.
a men,
T.
B.
p
Tranquillo ♩ = 70
(Ped.)

127
a - - - - - - - - men,

131
a - - - - - - - - men,

135
a - - - - - - - - - - - -
rit.
139
- men.
rit.